Local Men
and
Domains

Local Men
and
Domains

Two Books of Poetry
by
James Whitehead

University of Illinois Press
Urbana and Chicago

For Jack Marr, Glenn Ray, and Tom Royals
and for my brother, Jerry Whitehead
Local Men

———————

For Gen
Domains

Manufactured in the United States of America
P 5 4 3 2 1
This book is printed on acid-free paper.

Local Men was originally published in 1979
by the University of Illinois Press.

Domains was originally published in 1966
by the Louisiana State University Press.

Library of Congress Cataloging-in-Publication Data

Whitehead, James.
  Local men ; and, Domains.

  I. Whitehead, James. Domains. 1987. II. Title:
Local men. III. Title: Domains.
PS3573.H48A6 1987   811'.54   87-5096
ISBN 0-252-01443-X (alk. paper)

Contents

Local Men

A Local Man Remembers Betty Fuller   3

The Plain Story of Macintosh the White Cropper Who
Never Stopped Talking Until He Got to Death   4

In Neshoba County   6

After Reading *Beowulf* Again   7

About a Year after He Got Married He Would Sit
Alone in an Abandoned Shack in a Cotton Field
Enjoying Himself   8

He Remembers Figuring a Logic for the Life That
Went On the Summers He Cruised Timber   9

The Delta Chancery Judge after Reading *Aubrey's
Brief Lives*   10

He Records a Little Song for a Smoking Girl   13

The Narrative Hooper and L.D.O. Sestina with a
Long Last Line   14

He Remembers Something from the War   16

The Recently Sober Man's Prayer for Autumn   18

A Better than Average Boy Prays after Loving the
Afflicted Daughter and Wife   19

Doing Bidness   20

Nonce Sonnet as Epistle—A Local Man Begins to
Understand Why He and His Friend Failed to
Crash and Burn with the Good Women They
Encountered in a Distant Town   21

A Local Man Is Drunk but under Control in a Tonk
with Marginal Friends 22

Good Linemen Live in a Closed World 23

On Finding Her Out When He Comes In, Their
Children Fast Asleep After the Holiday Is Over 24

He Remembers How He Didn't Understand What
Lieutenant Dawson Meant 25

A Local Man Doesn't Like the Music 26

He Loves the Trailer Park and Suffers Telling Why 27

His Slightly Longer Story Song 28

The Travelling Picker's Prayer and Dream 29

I Write in a Peculiar Mood Unworthy of the Trust 30

A Better than Average Boy Reconsiders the Fact That
His Momma Taught Him Right from Wrong 31

For Berryman 32

For Gen 33

What the Chancery Judge Told the Young Lawyer
after a Long Day in Court 34

A Brief Review of *The Devils* 35

After Having Read Aloud Some Favorite Poems the
Local Circuit Judge Enjoys Fine Table Whiskey
and High Talk 36

Wherein the Lawyer from George County Recounts
Events Soon and Some Time After He Crossed
the Bar 37

The Leflore County Lawyer Recollects His Client
Sullivan 40

The Curious Local Banker After Having Read a
Recent Anthology 42

Having Gained Some Spiritual Ruthlessness but Still
    Confused by What Has Happened a Local Man
    Considers a Friend Who Died Alone   43

He Listens to His Brother Begin to Enjoy a Beautiful
    Social Woman at a Party   44

Some Better than Average Advice about Writing
    from the Elder Local Novelist Who Is a Craftsman
    of Sorts and Wise and Prolific   45

A Local Contractor Flees His Winter Trouble and
    Saves Some Lives in a Knoxville Motel Room   46

The Country Music Star Begins His Politics   47

Long Tour: The Country Music Star Explains Why
    He Put off the Bus and Fired a Good Lead Guitar
    in West Texas   48

For Our Fifteenth Anniversary   49

A Recently Recorded Picker Experiences a Complicated
    Sadness and Provokes Himself into a Prayer   50

Pay Attention, Son   51

The Alabama Man Remembers All He Can about
    the Battered Children and the Woman with Almost
    Perfect Skin in Mobile Seven Years Ago   52

Troubled in a Dallas Hotel He Remembers Lady
    Years Later   53

A Local Man Can't Handle the Lady's Problems   55

Trying to Explain a Bad Man to a Good Man at the
    Neshoba County Fair in 1971   56

Visionary Oklahoma Sunday Beer   57

Dealing with Mary Fletcher   58

A Local Man Ponders a Letter He Has Received
    from a Liberal Woman He Continues to Admire   60

A Local Man Estimates What He Did for His Brother
Who Became a Poet and What His Brother Did
for Him   61

Some Local Men after Their Election   62

Domains

Floaters   65

Two Voices   66

Delta Farmer in a Wet Summer   67

One for the Road   68

Common   69

A Local Man Goes to the Killing Ground   70

The Flood Viewed by the Tourist from Iowa   71

For Flannery O'Connor   72

The Opinion of an Interesting Old Man   73

The Young Deputy   74

McComb City, August, 1958   76

After Hours   77

Taking a Break   79

The Wreck   81

Desertions   82

The Zoo, Jackson, Mississippi, 1960   84

Swimming   85

The Lawyer   86

His Old Friend Who Sometimes Comes to Talk   88

The Politician's Pledge   89

On Hearing That the State Economic Council Believes
$5000 a Year for Every White Family Will Quiet
Things Down   90

Eden's Threat   91

Miracle Play   92

Tornadoes   93

Just North of Sikeston   95

Notes for a Homily: The Medieval Monk Broods Over
an Epic   97

Leavings   98

Kalma   99

For a Neighbor Child   100

My Son's Bad Dreams   101

My Elderly Cousin   102

One for the Sea   103

News Photo with a Hurricane Story   104

Overcoming Bad Weather   105

First Lecture   107

On the Lady's Clothes   109

Cul-de-sac   110

Words for the Sexual Revolution   111

Love Poem in Midwinter   112

For MM   113

Walking Around   114

For the Lady at Her Mirror   115

Domains   116

Local Men

Lord, if I judge 'em
Let me give 'em lots of room —
Tom T. Hall

With this I do not mean to propose
a peace treaty —
Emma Goldman

There is a disease of the human mind,
called the metaphysical tendency, that
causes man, after he has by logical
process abstracted the quality from
an object, to be subject to a kind
of hallucination that makes him take
the abstraction for the real thing —
Errico Malatesta

A LOCAL MAN REMEMBERS BETTY FULLER

Betty Fuller cried and said, Hit me.
I did. Which made her good and passionate
But Betty Fuller never came. Fate
Decreed that Betty Fuller would not see
The generosity a lively house
And loyal husband bring. She lost her mind
In Mendenhall. She got herself defined
As absolutely mad. A single mouse
Caused her to run exactly down the line
Of a wide road, running both north and south
With execrations pouring from her mouth.

She's out at Whitfield doing crazy time
And she can't possibly remember me
Among the rest. I'm satisfied she can't.

THE PLAIN STORY OF MACINTOSH THE WHITE CROPPER WHO NEVER STOPPED TALKING UNTIL HE GOT TO DEATH

By the time he quit talking and got to death
His eyes were clabbered and the Picayunes
Had scoured down his lungs and throat and nose—
He hardly had a sense left except for sound
To hear his own voice with.
He'd bellow, "To hell with it—noise and feel
Is all the humans need,"
And then he'd squeal and dig at his open fly.

The loud delight of hearing his cruelties
And venialities
Come back around his yard in raunchy circles—
Cat screams, rooster crows
And bitch howls—like all
The generations of animals he'd kept
And buried—was what he lived on mostly.
He chanted those fine incestuous memories
To anyone who got within earshot—
Someone a half mile down the road could hear
Himself addressed before he saw the old man
Boiling off through the heat
Alive with Macintosh's history—
In broad sunshine a voice more furious
For ears than brigades of Turks—
A redneck Odyssey afloat on air
Like brigantines across a wild catarrh—
A voice fired through light like Minié balls or flak . . .

Children walking the far ridge could hear the time
He won a hundred on a doped horse in Memphis
And how he lost it on the best damned rut
A single man can get
And worth the Yellow Dog—

You'd see him blindly pissing off his porch
And know he did it through the floor inside.
No way in the world to make his going pleasant,
Though finally his yelling did stop. He fell
From his steps the time
I was close enough to cheer on his story
That celebrated how he'd killed a neighbor's brother
For riding a colt to death—and the whole white sky
Was mad as hell to see it, the breaking down
Of anything as ravenous and mean as Macintosh.

Weeds grew up through the floor and reached the ceiling.
His shack filled up with humid foliage
And then collapsed into a green
That dominates the fields for miles.
Sawgrass and dock and bitterweed
Reek eyeless in the heat
And down the road the silences are eloquent.

IN NESHOBA COUNTY

He shoots his snooker standing straight up
Because he can't bend—poke shots
And mostly they're inaccurate—
But when one does work
It shakes the pocket
And shivers the fat he is sunk in.

God, how his trousers ride up his huge ass
And how his mother must have loved on him.

His pale skin bulges over his high-top shoes—
It is whiter even
Than his rolled down
Sheer socks that have red veins
Like blood with poison in it.
Because of politics I fear this man's pain.

AFTER READING *BEOWULF* AGAIN

How shall we bear the fury of this dream?

The Rose of Heaven is nowhere seen. No Devil
Builds the Fancy City. The creatures seem,
However terrible, the easy drivel
Shot from Sunday sets. In fact, they seem

From Disneyland—our mothers' eyes that swear
On sex—our fathers' honest hands that scream
Above our butts. Sorrow is everywhere
And the goddamned story is told in starts and fits

As if a man's whole life were simply fights—
Redneck Jocastas, Dragon Bankers, Tits
Gunning for Glory in the name of Sense. Nights!
The only light being devouring bad breath.

How shall we tolerate this human death?

ABOUT A YEAR AFTER HE GOT MARRIED
HE WOULD SIT ALONE IN AN ABANDONED SHACK
IN A COTTON FIELD ENJOYING HIMSELF

I'd sit inside the abandoned shack all morning
Being sensitive, a fair thing to do
At twenty-three, my first son born, and burning
To get my wife again. The world was new
And I was nervous and wonderfully depressed.

The light on the cotton flowers and the child
Asleep at home was marvelous and blessed,
And the dust in the abandoned air was mild
As sentimental poverty. I'd scan
Or draw the ragged wall the morning long.

Newspaper for wallpaper sang but didn't mean.
Hard thoughts of justice were beyond my ken.
Lord, forgive young men their gentle pain,
Then bring them stones. Bring their play to ruin.

HE REMEMBERS FIGURING A LOGIC
FOR THE LIFE THAT WENT ON THE SUMMERS
HE CRUISED TIMBER

One time a wildcat jumped from a tree, and once
We saw twelve snakes in a single day of work,
But mostly there was little more than the dance
Of flying insects on the sun—then back
To Woodville for a sorry meal and beer
And waitresses who loved the picture show
And probably a screw without much cheer.
I tried to understand what I should know.

I thought of phrases. *Natural weather* was one.
A slow mean life was another. Also *bad taste*.

Late at night the sun stayed on my skin
And the motel sheets were stiff, and my smoke was a waste
Unless by force of mind I figured breath
Goes back to the leaves, rounding out my death.

THE DELTA CHANCERY JUDGE
AFTER READING *AUBREY'S BRIEF LIVES*

1

I think of shame, embarrassment and crime

Rott with the rotten;
Let the dead bury the dead
And that for William Chillingworth, Divine,
Because he mostly died of syphylis.
I agree with Aubrey—
Dr. Cheynell was unkind to Chillingworth.

Old John Aubrey was a man of parts
And was a sot: *Sot that I am,* he often wrote.

2

All that rancor, all that plague and fire
And every reputation cheap as lice—
It boggles me the sort of life I know.

"As he laye unravelling in the agonie of death,
the Standers-by could hear him say softly,
I have seen the Glories of the world"—
Isaac Barrow was that decent man.

Moniti meliora We now have better counsel—
How I doubt that sentence!

3

Last week I fixed divorce for three young men
And each was wrong
Unworldly and unkind to his desperate wife.
Dumb as pig shit, each was terrified
Of anything his mother didn't know.

Our simple education softens teeth
And all their fathers bit their thickened tongues.
Their children never will
Strap on or see the glories of the world.

4
Who is the King of Chancery today?
Who can personify Sweet Equity
Now everything begins with common law?

My court is for insurance men who lose
And give their money out of policy
Because I contradict my style and rule
Almost exclusively
Against their company.
I will be re-elected.

5
A year ago there was a funeral,
The mistress to a friend,
And when the graveside nervous prayer was done,
His wife let go a scream:
No one to keep the bastard off of me!

He was gone for fifteen weeks alone
But never more than eighty miles from here
Doing business from his motel rooms.
He got back home and there was no reprieve.

6

Sometimes my few good friends with their good wives
And I with mine, we leave
Denying every province of our pain
For days of games and plays.

Sots all, we will maintain some glory for this world.

Smoking all that much has got her eyes
Pinched and a little lined—so the misery
Of cigarettes deserves a song. Prize
For doing anything, catastrophe
In small doses, smoke cuts into a face
Almost as deep as Benzedrine and booze.

Still she's a lovely girl in every place
Because she is so young. O she will lose
Her surfaces of head in love and time
Though all the rest stay smooth and be close-pored.
Her legs would make a blind man smile, and rime—
Her belly and the thing in sweet accord
Years from now will cry, Forgive, forgive
My cigarettes, I swallowed smoke alive.

THE NARRATIVE HOOPER AND L.D.O. SESTINA
WITH A LONG LAST LINE
for Leon Stokesbury

One fall not far from Ozark, Arkansas
A gentle sheriff saw a hairy man
Upon the berm—hairy in the extreme
This man was, but kindly from his bearded face.
He hunkered there upon the fading grass
And to the sheriff seemed entirely at peace.

It's wonderful to see a boy at peace
So much he seems to love our Arkansas,
Even if he's vagrant on the grass,
The sheriff thought, who was a decent man,
Although not one to wear a bearded face,
Which faces were to him at least a bit extreme.

Could be this boy's entirely extreme,
A hooper flipped on dope and not at peace
At all with Arkansas—he'd have to face
This hairy one near Ozark, Arkansas
To prove the Law is not the lesser man
Than one who is so fearless in the autumn grass.

And so the sheriff stopped his car, on the grass
And on the berm, in a state of mind extreme
For such a gentle and a decent man
Who lived in fact essentially at peace
With every normal man in Arkansas.
He parked, but showed some fear upon his razored face.

It was a moment all good men will face
In time, and man to man, on God's own grass—
We all must be in Ozark, Arkansas
Or somewhere just the same and as extreme
Some time, attempting to maintain the peace,
As honest sheriff or as gentle hairy man.

And so it was with our two friends. The man
Who had the hair on said, "Sheriff, your face
Suggests I've done some thing to break the peace
While taking of my ease upon the grass."
"I'm not exactly sure it's that extreme . . .
Are you a hooper?" the sheriff mumbled, then clearly saw

His man was nervous—"Boy, are you on grass
Or L.D.O.!" His face was now extreme.
"Peace, Sheriff," said the hairy man, "I'm no hooper—I'm
from Dumas, Arkansas."

In Kansas during the war
   my grandfather made a big thing
   of a car left out in our alley—
There's bullet holes and human blood
   so hurry up and eat your supper.
And the whole world would jiggle a little
   like Jello, when he was nervous.
Mother and grandmother were gone
   to the movies to see my father winning
   the war in Europe—grandfather
   never went to the movies or church
   and for the same reasons.
This is a lot like the real trouble
   your father is having in Germany,
   he said, as we walked past our victory garden
   then down our alley.

The things themselves were plain—
   a blue Nash and a windbreaker
   stiff with blood
   but I wasn't scared
   even by the stain itself
   until he told the story
   about how for some reason
   a hitch-hiker had murdered a farmer
   then left the car and jacket in our alley
   after dumping out the dead farmer
   in the woods of northern Arkansas.
About the time the police arrived
   I asked why in our alley?
He was the only father I had
   those long years during the war
   my mother was gone to in the movies.

Later that night mother and grandmother
scolded him for getting drunk
because they didn't know the things
behind the garden
and wouldn't until the morning news
that told another story
which was a lie grandfather said,
like Roosevelt.
Upstairs he staggered near the door
outside my room and close to my bed
where that night in a sweaty dream
I saw a German soldier
catching a ride
with my own father
in my own father's M-4 tank
that was standing out in our alley.

Send a cool day, Lord, and let me rest—let wind
Blow hard and the rain cease. My insect life
All summer long is rich and full. Offend
Their wings away. Sober as a butter knife
Please let me be, and that for morning bread.

A patient decency is what I want—
Much more chattering and I am dead.
Lord, am I bitten into sense, or bent?

Unlike nice birds they fly backwards, hover
Like helicopters. They don't pace so well
As geese or albatrosses. I'm no lover!
Drive insects down some sea! Diminish hell.
Strictly speaking, Lord, I live in fear.

I shudder as your beast and breathe fresh air.

A BETTER THAN AVERAGE BOY PRAYS
AFTER LOVING THE AFFLICTED DAUGHTER AND WIFE

Lord, the will to make small virtue stand!
Lord, my fear of her husband and father. Lord,
Those two incapable of her. My hand
Passed over her afflictions where were stored
The sadness and the need. Did I do right
Or cunningly or cruelly or wrong?

I have strange dreams wherein I have to mount
The bent creation—and there is a song
Whose bars sing harmony except one line
In the language of a keen of small pleasure.
She said, Thank you—I think that was just fine.

Husband and father will never measure
What she knows. Don't you agree? I want
Some peace in this. Please curse the ones who won't.

DOING BIDNESS
for William Harrison

Encourage the several small catastrophes
You suffer every day, especially
Abuse over the phone. Smile. Say cheese
While they are crying, Bastard! Shit! I see
Your point. Say that you see something, a point.

Outside small mountains exhale and the dead are warm,
Locked down in heavy August, don't worry rent.
Masts pop over the verge, pray for a storm
With organ music. Steerage is yourself.
The worst is yet to come. The phonecalls aren't.

Just one one day will stutter toward a laugh,
Alive within your office, forefinger bent
Against the trigger. Well, the round won't kill.
But, Christ, the noise, the noise is terrible.

NONCE SONNET AS EPISTLE—A LOCAL MAN BEGINS TO UNDERSTAND WHY HE AND HIS FRIEND FAILED TO CRASH AND BURN WITH THE GOOD WOMEN THEY ENCOUNTERED IN A DISTANT TOWN

You said the smart ones do it right away—
Even quicker than the dumb—but ours
Were in the middle distances, good girls
With normal minds and common debts to pay—
Rents and children in the second room,
Divorce and separation in their dreams—
No way, no way—and when that baby screams
You know the earth took more than a single day.

Why'd their husbands leave with them so warm?
Neither one would turn a good man down
Or deny the sensual request
If it's sincere. They do their decent best
And like it, too. Somebody did them harm
Then ran. A balanced woman requires charm.

A LOCAL MAN IS DRUNK BUT UNDER CONTROL
IN A TONK WITH MARGINAL FRIENDS

Her eyes are slightly clouded and sleepy dirt
Is up against her pitted nose on both sides
And her sour yellow mess has not been brushed
The hundred strokes that every lady knows—
It hangs down over her shoulders in coils
And her skin is like a baked potato peel's
Insides. I know
The man she's nourishing. He says he loves
The way she smells and when he gets drunk a little
He goes insane over how his woman is.

Lord, their nervousness—
Any Quaker's hour would be heaven to them—
Every man
With discipline and work to take pride in
Drives the bottle down his tender throat.
These skinny lovers in their bed make sounds
Exactly like Ezekiel's bones, but they,
Unlike the ancient vision, can't get up.
Their house I went to once is like a pen,
Sour mash and pork and sour grain.

Nothing takes shape here.
They only care for me because I pay . . .
They hate me for my pleasures in the rain
On nights I come to town . . .
They hate the easy horses of my dreams
And everything that goes
With children and money and a fancy wife.
Both have said I lead the easy life—
And there is no Christ of Gin to save them with
And God's own politics would be too late.

GOOD LINEMEN LIVE IN A CLOSED WORLD

Good linemen live in a closed world—they move
Inside themselves to move themselves against
The others and their violence—they give
To interior visions whole seasons no good sense
Would approve—their insides creak and groan, crying
A thing that's trapped along the line is shrill
And curious and wants out. Bodies playing
Laugh and dream to gain the massive will
Their trade requires. These men maintain, they attack,
They suffer repetition for years and years.
Part war and similar to art, their work
Is sometimes elegant. Inside their fears
At the closed center of one fear, they move
Quickly against themselves with a massive love.

ON FINDING HER OUT WHEN HE COMES IN, THEIR CHILDREN FAST ASLEEP AFTER THE HOLIDAY IS OVER

No way. No way. There's no reasoning
How conjugal the terrors are, the rage
These women feel against their men. The thing
Is gone. Old marriage like the persiflage

Of maiden aunts on dope is strictly mad.
We men grow facial hair for war again,
Repeating like Edwardians, Cad, Cad,
Emitting awful tropes that merely grin
Like the face she drew in the pumpkin pie.

I jog these rhythms in a dream, praying
Not to scream at her again, or cry,
Asking why my drunk tongue keeps dully saying
Not even children sleeping well are worth this,
And why no grace should make bad lovers kiss.

HE REMEMBERS HOW HE DIDN'T UNDERSTAND
WHAT LIEUTENANT DAWSON MEANT

Lieutenant Dawson said he'd known the girl
For fifteen years
But I couldn't read his face
Or his shaved head—
He said there's something cruel
About the way these people live—Disgrace
And Violence and Crime.
He made a list
That never added up to heavy grief.
Three times he opened up then closed a fist
And said he'd known she'd never have a life.

Outside the small and mean low-ceilinged room
Where she lay dead, her pretty body torn
And ruined by the shoe and stolen ring
Her boyfriend used,
Dawson freed a groan
That wasn't clearly out of sympathy—
Then said this is your basic tragedy.

A LOCAL MAN DOESN'T LIKE THE MUSIC

Those tunes don't recollect one memory
I ever had. Not one could call my name.
And when the music isn't company
It's time to go and time to change your mind.

I've been dissatisfied. My pretty wives
Were decent, warm, and wrong. My sons have played
It smarter than I did. My daughters' lives
Are better than their mothers'. They are good.

I love them all, but I don't love them well.
I've been dissatisfied to be alone,
The one sure way to make your bed in hell.

I'll change my mind. I'll like to where I've gone,
Whatever trailer park or motel room.
Alone or with some girl, I'll write a song.

HE LOVES THE TRAILER PARK AND SUFFERS TELLING WHY

A hopeful life is possible out here,
And sometimes nervous,
Though few of us will ever travel much.
Storms are what we fear.
Sometimes our metal homes are worse than thatch
Or mud huts or hide tents, when the wind comes.
Trailer Park Destroyed—a common line
Because nobody ever ties them down
The way suggested.

That's hopeful, true, a sign
Of basic piety, unworldliness
To help define the insane goings-on
You read about. Lives here are quite a mess.
We have a joke that goes, "We live in tin."

But still we have more fun than we do wrong.
We take a simple pleasure from the rain.

27

HIS SLIGHTLY LONGER STORY SONG

She was older, say, thirty-five or so,
And I was eighteen, maybe. She was dark
And musical, I thought, out of a book
I hadn't read, Louisiana slow,
A chance to get my ass shot off or grow
Up quickly, outdistancing the nervous pack
Of boys I ran with. I was green but trick
By trick she taught where innocence could go
When what I wanted happened. Innocence
Or ignorance? Or neither one? Or both?
She claimed she'd taken sweetness from my life.

She cried, imagining the pretty wife
I'd hammer with some grief. She said the breath
Of love—this kind—was mostly arrogance.
She'd drink and then she'd dance
Alone and naked to the radio.
She said I was her baby. I said no.
She said in time I'd throw
Away her memory. I knew she lied.
I said I loved her body, loved her pride.

THE TRAVELLING PICKER'S PRAYER AND DREAM

Lord, forgive our drinking. Forgive our dreams
Of decency we can't shake off. Sisters
Are involved, and mothers, say our screams
That wake the whole bus up, and ministers
We come from haven't helped.

The poor are moral
But none of us have rotten teeth. Our teeth
Are good, washed by salt water. Fancy coral
Grows and forms what's called a barrier reef—
But what we're up against we can't be sure

Unless it is the sea, and the sea's too big
To drink to, and the sea's also impure
As Eve's mouth on the apple or Adam's fig.
Lord, a picker's dreams should not be cursed.
Remember the souls in the last hard town we blessed.

I WRITE IN A PECULIAR MOOD UNWORTHY OF THE TRUST

Everybody in this house I love,
All of you, I know you memorized
And hold your faces.
Soon I'll claim I strove
To raise you not exactly victimized
And hope you live at least ninety years
With normal minds and understanding hearts—
Bruun, Kathleen, Eric, Joan, Philip,
Edward, Ruth, observe the strict defeats
A father suffers.

Your father is a tulip,
A withdrawn man who won't outgrow his fears
Of pleasant husbandry and ignorance.
Learn to avoid his awkward mental dance.

He's liliaceous to a fault. Say that
He fumbled daily in the words for it.

A BETTER THAN AVERAGE BOY RECONSIDERS THE FACT
THAT HIS MOMMA TAUGHT HIM RIGHT FROM WRONG

She did—also the chilly sweats of lust—
Although how she was sensitive was nice,
For Momma's pain was real and learned and blessed.
When Momma hugged you once, she hugged you twice.

And only criminals would say these things.
I qualify. I've done time on the farm,
Six months of decent work and sweet bird songs.
The guard just hit me once to break my arm.

Hey hey hey—and now I'm going straight
Because I love my wife and family.
Friend, I keep her off the boys and hate
Myself when I'm too soft on daughter. I

Would rather be unlike my daddy, Lord.
He was a good man. Momma called him good.

FOR BERRYMAN

Considering how casually his doom
Gets off, considering all the sweats, Fuck it
Comes to mind. A fellow builds his room
And voices natural enough to fit
The insane time he does, then takes a dive . . .

Piss on the butcherman, piss on the suet
Tied in winter sacks. Birds are alive
But Big John isn't and every head has got

Its rat.
      He's company for Mistress Anne—
Who fed on now feeds the cruellest scholarship
While every lover fiddles with his chin—
Reasoning, we call for booze, the whip
To make our shitty bodies right. God damn!

No one will soon rise up like Berryman.

FOR GEN

A nuptial mass was what we couldn't do
Since I was from the Presbyterians
And you a daughter of the Irish nuns
In Yazoo City.

Loss was always true
For us—the postcard of the scourged Jesus you carried
The day we met—the case for rectitude
I'd buried in a tonk. For years we tried
For virtues we were taught, and then we married.

Children—Lord, we've born children like a pope
In spite of every secular device,
Including three at once. Wife, we are dated—
Love, these years we have excessively mated,
Though not for God. Notice the wink of Christ
So naturally the body is our hope.

WHAT THE CHANCERY JUDGE TOLD
THE YOUNG LAWYER AFTER A LONG DAY IN COURT

Name the widows and divorcees you know,
Then recollect their comments on the dead
Or gone they speak of when the lights are low.
Lord, that their memories of love are sad.
Lord, how the simple sky is always blue
And the spring grass green, while the poor marriage bed
Grows colorless, because no love stays true.
Friend, they want their sex back bad and red.

Men and women share relief sometimes,
Especially when their serious hopes break out—
We learn all evidence is ruined dreams—
We find most things are proved outside our court.

Her husband never drank a day of work.
We knew all day her time was bleak, Christ, bleak.

A BRIEF REVIEW OF *THE DEVILS*

Brueghel's wheels outside Chirico's walls
And lots of bad sex inside. It's quite a story
Although quite simple—plague is clearly glory
And the convent gleams with fancy shower tiles
Not unlike a modern locker room.

Jesus! the ample pain the eye can stand—
Lopped limbs, the eternal whipping of the big gland—
It's all about a natural man, his doom—
Bye, bye, blackbird, and the nun has an icon neck—
Louis and the Cardinal are weird
And funny. Their Power is unafraid
To kill a city for Real Politik.

It's obvious. There's one straight dick in town:
Break his bones, burn his ass, bring him down.

AFTER HAVING READ ALOUD SOME FAVORITE POEMS THE LOCAL CIRCUIT JUDGE ENJOYS FINE TABLE WHISKEY AND HIGH TALK

Those who fall down because of law and love,
The proper indiscretions of our race,
I'll praise and justify. Old sin will thrive
On what I say, remembering her face,
And laugh at how we always were so fancy—
In fact, had Calvin's spies caught us on film
They would have cut their eyes and called it filthy.

White people suffer a peculiar carnal dream.
White educated people suffer love
In the old way, whatever that way is.

She and I while fucking sometimes strove
To understand the loving of the ages.
Our joining recollected history.
Five times in four sweet days we both went free.

WHEREIN THE LAWYER FROM GEORGE COUNTY
RECOUNTS EVENTS SOON AND SOME TIME
AFTER HE CROSSED THE BAR

1

Red is naturally a bourbon man—
In fact the best I've known to shake a fifth
Of green Jack riding
The semi-tropical backroads of George
The summer Tucker won the D.A. race
And say, "Watch out for the higher altitudes—
They make the whiskey work too goddamned well."

The head-on chicken farm was on the rise
In George, where if the rain blows from the south
You sink completely in the Gulf of Mexico.

2

We drove and drank all afternoon the day
That Tucker won his race
Because politically he was our man—
We shot some cans before we left Red's place,
Then passed by all the ponds and creeks in George
That hold the rusting John Deere tractor parts.

Even after Red has got it shaken
Sometimes it's hard to drink it straight in George.

Tucker was our man
And he would surely win.

3

It wasn't bourbon that caused the two of us
To bury tractor parts
The afternoon the hurricane came through—
The wind and rain beat inland from the Gulf
And drowning tractor parts

37

I learned some strange law
On the same roads we drove when Tucker won.

It was your gin that Red went crazy on
The night the storm came through. Pressure
Made him steal those tractors from the John Deere man.

4
I got a call from Betty saying Red
Was sitting on the biggest one at dawn—
I better come on home with my new law
And reason with her man
Who wasn't often reckless with their life.

I did. I said confess. Return it all—
Though Red had by that time ruined one—
He'd torn it down to parts and nuts and bolts
And said confession never helped a thief
In George: "*This* is not your killing. *I'm a thief!*"

5
And he was right. I took to wrenches, mad
As hell to realize the hurricane
Was bending trees like switches at the brake.
Also, the Sheriff wasn't anybody's fool.
Tear the damn things down! Fill the truck!
We did. Our hands got bloody in the rain—
Though the rain was how we got the time to work
Against the law.
Red shook his Jack and drove
While I threw tractors part by part into the water.

6

We got it done in time, then faced the Sheriff
Where the water poured across the road.
He had his side and we had ours.
He said we had the tractors—
We said we never did—
But he was pissed enough to try to ford
Which got him swept away
And drowned at Little's Dam
Down from the chicken farm.
Red dove three times, recovered him, and cried for days.

7

I still see Red in dreams
Cold sober with the Sheriff by one arm—
He's yelling and waving me out of the pickup's bed—
And I still hear illegal wind like pain
Alive in every pine.

We worked to save the Sheriff where he lay
Until the water reached to pull us in . . .

It's on election day we drive the roads
Drunk to fancy tractor parts beneath
Low water lost in ponds and lost at Little's Dam.

THE LEFLORE COUNTY LAWYER
RECOLLECTS HIS CLIENT SULLIVAN

He chose that dynamite
Because the war was why she loved on him—
She loved to hear about those quilted coats
The Chinese soldiers wore—
And she went wild in split-row cotton fields.
He said she'd run off toward the brake butt-naked
Yelling she's on fire for all of him.

He never questioned her vitality
Or her smooth skin and lovely yellow hair
He followed over all those slick dance floors.
Cascades and beer bubbles and little lights
Eased his memories
Of winters in a cold Korean trench.
Garters and hose and split briefs
Hid the dark side of what she had to have
And what he gave for a long time before
He realized how sick and wrong it was.

My client Sullivan
Knelt at the edge of the woods
With those sticks of dynamite
Spread out around his boots
And studied the house he'd worked to build for her
Exactly like a slab of marble cake
Beneath a lover's moon—
Something generally fine that rots your gums
And makes the last blond curls come falling out
Unless you mix in something normal with it.
There wasn't any reason to abuse
And abuse the body he loved.
That made him sick, but not so sick as the stories
About the ones who would.

Sullivan got to his feet—he stood straight up
And lobbed them in exactly where she was.
He wasn't confused at all
By the cries of the nightbirds
Or the fog that rose from the slough.
Those explosions tore it down—those five
Explosions gave her a final perfect beating
While clapboard and glass flew around like popcorn.
He did exactly what he had to do.

THE CURIOUS LOCAL BANKER
AFTER HAVING READ A RECENT ANTHOLOGY

Their poetry is strange and wonderful
And surely using chemicals with them
Would be a good time, fresh and fanciful,
Especially with those thin girls in a wild room
Where violent gestures wouldn't be allowed,
Although I think in fact they are afraid
The ways I am.

Dead—I see the dead
In many of the images they braid
Into their long hair. They wear the fine bones
Of mad grandmothers, wear the skins of aunts
As if they know what skin and bones will mean.
They wear their poems the way brokers wore hats
Before the culture changed. But that's O.K.
Everybody means to die at play.

HAVING GAINED SOME SPIRITUAL RUTHLESSNESS
BUT STILL CONFUSED BY WHAT HAS HAPPENED
A LOCAL MAN CONSIDERS A FRIEND
WHO DIED ALONE

He was a vain man and died courageously,
Except calling him vain defines the fault
As less than what it was. I've come to see,
Now he's in the ground, how he never meant

Much more than entertainment by the love
He gave us all. His death makes love a word
To be confused by. Mean, he had to prove
Our sympathy alone. His solitude

Toward the end was fancy cruelty—
His wife, his children and his friends shut out,
He would achieve the full catastrophe,
As sailors faced where Ocean Sea must quit.

Busy in the torn rigging of his heart,
He died, I hope, in a calm mortal sweat.

HE LISTENS TO HIS BROTHER BEGIN TO ENJOY
A BEAUTIFUL SOCIAL WOMAN AT A PARTY

My brother's voice is very close to mine—
It rumbles from a baritone to a bass
Then hits the high notes in a country song.
Older, I almost hear without disgrace
Our nervousness inside all heavy talk.

I stand to hear myself bend to a lie
When a social woman ranges from the track
Our wilderness allows. (I've heard him cry
Out of confusion many nights at home
A long, long time ago.) He has regained

Composure in the thicket of her dream.
He turns a line that's absolutely charmed.
He likes the sound of her. He hardly falters.
At best we sing exactly like our father.

SOME BETTER THAN AVERAGE ADVICE ABOUT WRITING
FROM THE ELDER LOCAL NOVELIST
WHO IS A CRAFTSMAN OF SORTS
AND WISE AND PROLIFIC

Some other subjects lie around, but fear
And overcoming fear are favorites—
Especially the overcoming. Hear
The nervous ventricle. Count up the nights

Courageous lovers live through during years
Of marriage and their children. Victories
Over the foul mouth, drink and idle tears
Out of the 19th Century will please

Your decent readers. Make him catch his breath.
Then make her pull the covers to her chin.
Readers who read in bed do not love death.
Good readers like their stories almost clean.

Your books dropped to the floor, they touch each other—
You've written well enough to make them bother.

A LOCAL CONTRACTOR FLEES
HIS WINTER TROUBLE
AND SAVES SOME LIVES
IN A KNOXVILLE MOTEL ROOM

Nobody is dead yet and won't be. Right.
Right. Right. Because I am a snake aware
Of wintertime. Out there is a hard night
To study, friends, deciding I'm still fair
Enough to keep the Remington locked up.
My dreams are bloodier than movies, buddy,
Because I'm wise enough to hide the clip.
You should be sainted when you quit on ready.

Mother is gone, dead as an animal,
And Daddy is strange—he fishes in the rain—
And my ex-wife, men, will defeat you all.
Everybody longs for where they began
Or where they've never been, you better believe.
You better believe we all end up alone.

THE COUNTRY MUSIC STAR BEGINS HIS POLITICS

There are no deadlier Americas
Than those I see from stages where I work,
And over coffee in the bad cafes,
Which is how everyone is going broke
Investing in good times and sentiment
Which pays my wages.
                         Squandering their love
The size of death and a revival tent
A troubled pride is what I have to give.

Whatever else they want they hardly say,
And I don't either. I am paid to strum
And make up songs that help grown children play.
The thing I do has prospered and gone wrong.
Lord, we are multiplied and we mean well.
There's murder in the darkness I can't kill.

LONG TOUR:
THE COUNTRY MUSIC STAR EXPLAINS WHY
HE PUT OFF THE BUS AND FIRED
A GOOD LEAD GUITAR IN WEST TEXAS

The day I put him off the sun outside
The cafe window didn't have a mind
For anything but lighting up a road
Covered with hair and plates and guts and blood
Of animals. He always counted them.
In the jump seat he'd count the creatures dead
Three hundred miles until we'd stop at noon.
He'd add them up in a notebook he carried.
He said that eggs were almost perfect food.
He said he'd met the man that ate the toad.
His breakfast stories went from fair to bad:
A couple wanted children, tried and tried,
But they got fur and nails like little wings
And every time the little baby died:
Then once again they tried
While making love to all our pretty songs —
She gave her man a watch, he gave her rings,
And God forgave their wrongs,
And it was born alive, a nine-pound eye.
I fired him for that. And he was good.

FOR OUR FIFTEENTH ANNIVERSARY

I'm here for the duration, Lord,
In a big house with seven children—
Bless this place
And shower sensuality upon
The adults in it.
We have been in love five times
These fifteen years, a good marriage

And shower sensuality upon
Our children as they come of age—
Teach us to live with what they know—
Point out right times for perfect rage—
Sons, daughters, let them grow.

And thank you for the company of Gen,
So calm in bed, so often fun.

A RECENTLY RECORDED PICKER EXPERIENCES
A COMPLICATED SADNESS AND PROVOKES HIMSELF
INTO A PRAYER
for Carl Launius

There's pleasure in success. God knows there is.
For like the good man said, "Success is Salvation"—

Savage beyond repair or otherwise,
There is a ballad song, for sure, some creation
That tells exactly how awful things are—
True. There are songs and there are story songs
Similar to the cold lungs of a star.
A poor boy needs the very thing he sings.

Hidy ho—Hidy ho—the dead
In Nashville kill the virtue that we do—
Salvation, Lord, is growing in my head,
And I am frightened, Lord, to find what's new.

I saw a country woman yesterday
Whose throat was gone, whose features were all clay.

PAY ATTENTION, SON
for Tom Royals and Sarge West

The things I've said were meant for praise
And I certainly never called you a liar.
All I did say was
It isn't possible in fact
To knock down flying animals
With a cotton boll—
And don't describe trajectories
Again. It's a damned good story,
Maybe the sort we have to have
To survive—
But it never happened—
And I know your daddy is stone deaf
And I'm sure it is his true belief
His word is all that killed that dog
Your mother spotted on the ridge—
I know that dog was killing chickens
And maybe did come howling in
To die without much blood. Maybe
It did flop down and die at his feet—
And I know he didn't see or hear
Your brother fire from the porch
At the same time
He slapped his old hat across his knee
And demanded, yes, in a voice to break
The meanest heart,
Death from the beast.
I'm sure he's positive that age
Has blessed him with a final power.
All I said was I don't believe
Your brother ever hit a dog
With a 22 at 500 yards
And I'll be glad to tell him to his face.
He missed or fell short.

THE ALABAMA MAN
REMEMBERS ALL HE CAN
ABOUT THE BATTERED CHILDREN
AND THE WOMAN WITH ALMOST PERFECT SKIN
IN MOBILE SEVEN YEARS AGO

Mostly the fat one remains inside my head
Because he was most bloody of them all
And was afflicted in his mind.
                                    My dread
Of what his people mean is terrible.

A damaged sister beat upon the door
I was involved behind.
                              Forgive me, Lord,
Those children crying got me off the floor
Whereon sweet love had almost shot us dead.

Continuing—I'm there for normal sin
With a woman with almost perfect skin.
She said, "We'll drive them to Emergency,"
Who were no kin to her or kin to me.

Above the pines the simple moon was bright.
After they were stitched, we said goodnight.

TROUBLED IN A DALLAS HOTEL ROOM
HE REMEMBERS LADY YEARS LATER

1

Lady—that fine old religious name
　　suggesting the late whimperings of birdcall
　　across the August cotton fields
　　and the vague lace of nylon panties
　　known on the moonlit seventh green
　　of moist grass at the Rosedale Country Club—
Lady—Lady—
　　you were so excellent in the blankets of humid morning
　　or to be exact, false dawn
　　and a long time after Rufus sang
　　"Danny Boy" for the last time
　　crying until our souls were warm and dark
　　rolling on the moonlit seventh green
　　(O dangerous banner, O strange device)—
So why within kind memory should I rebuke your gifts and
　　graces?

The tolerant river stars
　　have never judged you poorly—
But then of course the river stars make fools
　　and the weather was awful the next day.

2

All that afternoon the sun fell in
　　your momma's gin drink at poolside—
Your momma kept on saying
　　I think I mostly love summer because of
　　these gindrinks out here at poolside—
Except I'm fairly sure she said *boo-sad.*

Boo-sad! I feared the meaning of boo-sad.

53

Insight comes hard
   in summer lawn chairs at boo-sad
   with those fine old gindrinks in your hand—
   with the glistering heat roiling ghostly
   over the poisoned cotton fields—
And in that boiled twilight, a spectre,
My living father among the waves saying
   They all end up like their mothers, Son—
   study her mother close, Son.

And alas though you, Lady, were thin then
   as a strand of kudzu vine from a high tree,
Your momma wasn't.
                    She was a pear
With the big end turned up
   with toothpick legs that finally quit
   in thick feet she'd stuck in cherry sandals.

She kept on saying she was fond of me
   because *most boys these days and times*
   are raised thoughtless and basically wrong
   and haven't got whole afternoons
   to simmer a little drunkenly out here at boo-sad
   with me and Lady and Daddy.

3
I wanted to believe you favored Daddy
   who listened to grand opera
   and loved money and Tennyson
   and flying his Piper Apache under the Greenville bridge
   with your new friends, including me—
Because any man who loves to dive his plane to just above
   the fiery river—*pointillé* sun from Arkansas—
   intoning *Maud* until he's passed beneath the thing—
Can't be all bad, nor can his daughter.

A LOCAL MAN CAN'T HANDLE THE LADY'S PROBLEMS

Lady, I'd rather face my worse faults
Ten times in one day,
Even how I break out on friends
And those dreams of mine that kerosene
The neighbors' cats,
Than listen to your son's fears
And how you hate your husband.
I'm selfish. They weaken me.

After how he can't keep his food down
And after how your old cock with a pelt
Like a puma's is shacked up with his typist in the mountains,
God, I suck on my lips for hours—
I stare down my own boy's body and see my wife there.

Lady, I can't give you what you want.
I will not reason
Backwards through your life,
My little wisdoms sweating from each pore
And every convolution of my brain
A trough for small-time modern lecheries—
You're beautiful—
Go away.

TRYING TO EXPLAIN A BAD MAN TO A GOOD MAN
AT THE NESHOBA COUNTY FAIR IN 1971

Just because he fights dogs
And got in on the famous murders
Doesn't mean he'll kill you if
You walk up to his orange face and say
You're all hide and cruel inside and out.

He might just listen for where you come from.
He might just have his daddy's political sense
And say for a fact you Delta men
Lost power fifty years ago.

He might just twist an eye up and say
The niggers are riding you boys now,
And if you shunt or say something nervous,
Then, he might, at just that point,
Assault your body and break your face.

VISIONARY OKLAHOMA SUNDAY BEER
for Clarence Hall and Jane Cooper

The small window opened. I asked for the six-pack
I paid for, then saw the women playing pool
In the loud and common light where ball and stick
Have always met.
                    The oldest on a high stool

Was big as a mound but wasn't simply fat.
She glistened and shouted—she was having fun
With all the other Indians—each one great
With child in a way to make that bulb a sun.

All fancy with no men around, they played.
Hey, let me in is what I think I said.
I meant of course to ask where are your men
And what of pageantry and life and death?

Her break shook me and a brown arm closed down
A show I would have stayed a season with.

DEALING WITH MARY FLETCHER

1

Bolton Howard never served his time
Or anything. But he was strictly gifted
At dancing on a bill—
And thick as any pig he had three wives
Who if the word is right
Never saw him naked
And never wanted to.
He started with a ruined pulpwood truck
And once he wrecked his car and killed his child
By Mary Fletcher. He cried but didn't drink,
Which is insane,
Then sold his trailer park and went to hell.

2

After Mary Fletcher everything
Is pale, the story goes,
But no one gives details.
I used to watch her study clothes she bought
As if they might be fancy groceries.
She never tanned, for all the sun she took,
Who was as sensitive as gardening.
She married twice
And had good friends who always kept their tongues
Except to shudder when her name came up.
They never smiled.
I saw her buy three summer dresses once.

3

Hugo Lafayette Black
Once praised the legal mind of Albert Fletcher.
Judge Fletcher's opinions were written carefully
And his hedges were high as a goal
Because his troubled wife, a Methodist,
Was given to public tears for little reason—

And they never practiced anywhere but here,
And he raised his daughter almost by himself.
His wife before she died
Wrote a classic work on evidence
He took no credit for.
He wore a Panama and thick glasses.

4
I think all history
Revolves around my wife
Who says my head is like a ball of twine
I rarely use,
Or tape I lick until I gag. Her eyes
Are careless after life
But comforting in love,
And when I talk too much she won't put out.
Howard and the Fletchers piss her off.
I give her flowers twice a year, a brick
For Valentine's.
I give it in a sack.

5
Sometimes confusion in a private sorrow
Breaks a man. Davis is precisely that.
He was Mary's friend
But never came to much,
Considering the money he started with,
And Tulane Medical
And then a Jackson practice up until
Her child was killed. Connections are obscure.
He fell apart—
He lost his steady hand
Except for tying flies. He does that well
And writes pulp novels by another name.

A LOCAL MAN PONDERS A LETTER
HE HAS RECEIVED
FROM A LIBERAL WOMAN
HE CONTINUES TO ADMIRE
for John Little

She writes to say I am a radical,
Writing cursive, stretching her long mad hand
Straight up and down in such a way to fill
One yellow page torn from a legal pad.
She says my root is better than my tree—
Deep living root but very little trunk,
No complicated leaves, no canopy
Creating shades for squab and pleasant drink.

God knows exactly what the woman means.
Picnics? She writes I am a radical.
Lord, she is lovely, she is fed on dreams
And one time praised my green convertible.

Also, she says I am a sober mole—
No brilliant bird—I am a mole, a root.

A LOCAL MAN ESTIMATES WHAT HE DID FOR HIS BROTHER WHO BECAME A POET AND WHAT HIS BROTHER DID FOR HIM

I shot the chicken in the tree above
Where Herbert stood howling after I'd shot.
Bitterly he cried so loud of feathers Love
Itself became involved. Lord, lord, the fit
He threw was terrible. He said his head—
His sacred head—was daubed for poetry—
He said my cruelty would make him mad—
He said it was a ritual catastrophe.

Herbert was splattered with old chicken blood
And pink feathers from eyes to knees. He said
Later, twelve years later, that he was sad
He'd frightened me. Within a month he died.
On his deathbed he reached out for my hand
And said we come from where we get the wound.

SOME LOCAL MEN AFTER THEIR ELECTION
for President Jimmy Carter

They are suspicious now in the strange air
The morning after election. They are troubled
And sobering, afraid of their first beer.
They are responsible—they know they've gathered
Responsibility. Of this they're sure.
And they know responsibility is work.

They think of work and then they think of war.
They're less afraid and swallow their first drink,
Which isn't beer, is whisky. They're not broke.
Their new responsibility is good

And different and possibly no trick.
By now it's possible they're not too bad—
It is possible to be responsible
Away from war and the more terrible.

Domains

Floaters

Dallas Tanksley would run up on our yard
As skinny and fairly goodnatured as ever to say
His Daddy had spotted a floater, come and see . . .

Floaters were drowned people, turgid, not hard,
Surfacing around the bend about twice a year,
And usually a Negro from St. Louis
Bringing a stern sight down to all of us
In the country where only the deaths of the aged were clear.

My father said they jumped from the Barracks Bridge,
Being poor and debtors to boot and deeply in love
With something he never explained just then. Like a glove
Full of mother's cold dishwater, or maybe fudge
Left out a week and getting whitish from sugar
Crystals, they were pulled onto our sand bar.

Two Voices

Taggart says he gives them what they want—
They come to him in the night blind drunk and broke,
And he sews them up free, without a shot.
With his coarse thread he has the art to raise
Great scars from ear to ear, and he does just that—
It's part of a ritual they've done for years.
"I send them proud to the fields and gins," he says.
"With their heads pulled back that way, those bucks are grand,"
He says. "They brag after all we did it raw."

Thompson says you can hear their cries to the creek,
And he nearly objects, believing the fish in their way
Are offended—or at least that so much yelling
Can make a cat hook-shy, and anyhow
It's always Saturday night and Sunday morning
After the tonk fights and when he fishes.
"And not only that," Thompson says, "it's giving
Sorry dreams to my children." And almost angry:
"You'd think a doctor and all, he'd think of his neighbors."

Delta Farmer in a Wet Summer

Last summer was hot and dry, a better time—
Two cuttings at the dock and two knocked up
In the fields, and a crop to fill the wagons full.
There were prime steaks and politics at night,
Gin to nine and bourbon after that—
By God, we raised some handsome bales and hell,
Then went to New Orleans as usual.

But now it rains too long, too little sun
To stop the rot. Rain beats down on the roof
At night and gives sad dreams—black bolls—
And the Thunderbird will have to go. You can smell
It on the evenings, like the smell of a filthy
Bed, or wasted borrowed money, the stink
Of a bloated dog when finally the water's down.

. . . in California they say it's dry.
They irrigate consistently, don't count
The weather in when going to the bank,
And that's damned smart, except they've got no woods
Or sloughs to crowd the fields, and dogs get killed
But rarely drown—and I think our bitch, stretched hide
And stench, contains the element of
        chance a Christian needs.

One for the Road

Night full and the click of the lighter after love
    is almost kind, and careless, too, like the laugh
    I leave with the sullen bills. And that's the way
    it is, if not the way it ought to be,
    down this Memphis road . . .

I ought not pay, I know,
    but your way of going is easier than most—
    and even now, after I pull first drag,
    you're not half bad, and next to the rig you're the best
    of love I've got. You're a little soft in the pooch—
    but hell, I'm not a Natchez cock myself . . .

And it's not your legs or hair, God knows, not those,
    not easy things to get your mind around—
    it's your way of washing after all's got done,
    and something like fun among the common sounds—
    nails split, teeth gapped, who gives a damn . . .

And then the soft of loss with the coming sun,
    when you sleep me off like a dream almost of sin.

Common

More often than not my wife holds common sway
Over common things—and yet not commonly—
Like my fancy aunt flung *common* to my dismay
Against a friend of mine one day.

                        "He,
That Tanksley boy down by the river, is *common*—
All of them are common, every last Tanksley
There ever was." And that meant Dallas Tanksley
And Dallas Tanksley's solid mother who ran
For sheriff once to try and get good done.

My wife has yet to seek a public office—
And her children have never gone hungry—but I'm sure
She would, if she felt she should—if any face
In our house showed common need, or plain despair.

A Local Man Goes to the Killing Ground

They formed the ritual circle
of Chevy trucks. Tracks were there,
worn tires, the still prints in the mud
and thin grass. My light could barely suggest
the glare that fell on the men they killed.

It was an intimate thing—
all of them drawn in so close
they didn't bother with guns
or the normal uses of the knife.
It was done with boots.

I walked around that quiet place
and tried to reclaim the energy
that must of course remain in the earth.
It keeps the truth to itself
as they will, when they stride out of court.

By then it was all grey, false dawn—
and I thought it was like stomping
a fetus in the womb, a little
skin between the killers, the killed,
for the dead were curled in their passive way.

The Flood Viewed by the Tourist from Iowa

They paddled the street as fast as rowboats can,
To fetch back to the Parlor the Negro dead:
Embarrassment . . . that made no sense. A flood—
It was a flood, seven inches of rain
Through a single span of day and night, and all
In trouble just about the same. But still,
When word of the bodies came, the Public Will
Was wonderfully active. It was like Plague Call.

I suppose there was something ancient in it,
Men fearing the dead will walk, or maybe swim . . .

You should have seen those white men hurry to it . . .
None of the Negroes seemed nearly so grim
About it. In fact, one black, with a strange wit,
He sang a Freedom Song, hanging from a limb.

For Flannery O'Connor

Hell, you know we have to see some god
In the weeds, and a little botched with all that sun.
Like the town drunk or idiot or killer
He keeps on coming for dinner like a friend
We can't remember *where he knew our brother* . . . ?
Gobbles the chicken. Says, "I'm the one—
I'm the one Billy done in, and you—
You got to pay like you was him."   Billy!

Christ, we hadn't seen that fool for years—
Him with his teeth and all his crazy fears
If he stayed at home he couldn't have his fun . . .
Your freak stays on the place until he's through
With us. Insults. Rapes the women. Breaks
The mower. Weeds. Weeds. Weeds. Shouting—
"That sunnavabitch Billy, he's the one . . .
And I'm doing it all for *your* sakes . . . for your sakes!"

The Opinion of an Interesting Old Man

It's plain damned hard to lose yourself these days . . .
or at least you can't the clean way you once could . . .
gone for a week without boiled water and food,
then turning up in town misunderstood

with the whole place mad because they'd planned to say
nice things when sure you wouldn't come their way
again. It's a crying shame the way they're rude
enough to hunt you down within a single day

and just before you get that taste of fear
and just before you feel you're about to pray.
You hear them thrashing through the brush, when you're nude
with love of being lost. They think you're crude

if you plead you'd like to stay. They always intrude
like parents who are appalled by curious play,
and they trade with the oldest lie: "It's for your good,
dear friend. We've come to help you out," they say.

And out you go. Be sure they knew you would.
Be sure they'd rather have you alive than dead.

The Young Deputy

It was Leroy Smith we meant to find
in the slough, the old river, with hooks
but didn't. It was two others, or halves
of two, the big man's torso, the small
man's thighs, which made the sheriff sick
in the boat. It wasn't one man no matter
how hard he tried . . .

Eaten by fish was one answer.
Maybe gar. Drowned, with rope
still strung from the thick wrist, and a little
chain around the bottom's ankle.

(considering conflicting reports
of disappearance from various places
they might have been a dozen men)

Then it got to be a joke about
the burial: one grave or two,
since they'd got fixed as a single thing
in everybody's mind. Smith,
he never came to light, and it seemed
to figure that the one good grave
could somehow cover all three—and more,
said a few with furious souls.

There'd be, I thought, if things were right,
a fine day of picnicking,
preaching to a big mixed audience,
and in the nearest pine one buzzard,
glossy, hunkering, with a confused gaze.

McComb City, August, 1958

This town is silent. No wind
All day would cross the balustrade
And now in the streets the night
Dogs are gay and on parade,
Mad with an old moon.

I hear them begin to whine their thin curses
Against all signs of rain.
I watch them pad toward dawn where rage is.

After Hours

. . . of course of course there are those fat mother-lovers
who shoot guns and talk all hours (me sometimes)—
and the ones who make it a way of life watch out
for them. Noisy boys who never liked
their decent brothers and never liked hard work
much better—their monkeyshines, their wrecked Fords
and dirty women make them think they're big men.

But look at them at peace in honest houses now,
where the serious wrecks are with words—a busted participle
the compound fracture, the wife's bleeding heart
from his curse like a knife.

They claim three dead on the road—one girl—and really
crow their griefs in the raw hours, their past
and sin the staple of talk, as grease and bread
is their regular food, their tripe . . .

. . . so they hunt like marines in season and buy seatbelts—
so they dream of the bitch who wet the grass with blood
back then, remembering all, like their war or their one
best game—so they stare like cocks down a line
drawn on the chicken yard—show welts a buddy gave.
I'd say it's right to call them men.

And one more thing before I go—but quieter:
we all had better go easy on the lately reformed.
Everything in anyone that comes to grips with anything
has something to be said for it.
I know you've noticed my ring.

Taking a Break

Taking a break to smoke
We rested on a ridge
And Wyatt finally said
That in these woods were ghosts,
Slave dead and bad
Classicists who gave
Them Greek and Roman names.

He'd seen some stones the year
Before: *Plato, faithful*
Slave of Royal Green;
Marcus . . . such as that.
He said this stand was their dream
And far more civilized
Before we came to count trees.

He told how spirits stay
Because of violence
Done on the man's body,
How they stay confused
Around their old place
Until someone explains
Their killer has died too.

Our Picayunes made wraiths,
And it wasn't his way to joke—
But he wasn't afraid: "Ghosts—
But I'm not afraid. No more
Than snakes." And we didn't fear snakes.
They were common, and
We had our boots and razor

Blades—heavy khakis.
You can always bleed
Against a snake, and it seemed,
Hearing Wyatt talking
Flatly of ghosts around,
That something similar
Would certainly do for them.

The Wreck

One night just out of the woods
I came on a wreck, or what seemed
To be a wreck—the car
In the field was upside down,
The wheels still turning around,
And in the car, piled upside
Down, was the smiling driver
Whose body still seemed sound.

He opened his old Ford door
And crawled straight through the weeds
To where I nervously stood—
"Get up (if you can)," I said.
And he did. "I got my pride,"
He said: "Christ, how she ride!"
He grinned and tested his legs:
"She stays over there," he said,

"And I better, by God, start walking,"
And pointed toward a shed
Not far away, where the light
Was burning . . . his wheels still turning . . .

Desertions

Among books and tools some miles
From town, he gardens a little and speaks
Of her return:

My spirit describes the genuine
Concern a dear friend holds, as one
Might hold a tender bulb for planting.
Hers was a rout of sense, the sort
A child commits on pilfered wine,
An antic attitude for which
A plot of time must be set out
That growth become secure . . .

His trowel cuts a cup of mulch
To fix in the smallest window box:

Decay is studied or the heat
Destroys the thing it feeds—organic
Matter, of course, is best to raise
The famous beauty of the rose.

He smiles as if romantic lines
Could call rain down upon his plants:

You often praised her body's grace
And her wit, but when she left
She cried out foolishly
And tore off terribly gawkily . . .

And on through dinner his talk of flowers
Love and wine, until I free
Myself with the common excuse
And pass her rooms where the drawers
Are still open like stunned mouths.

The Zoo, Jackson, Mississippi, 1960

This zoo is a naked place;
Beasts of summer lodge
With habitants from ice;
Here the odd and poor

Of every kingdom come
To sample fear, where bar
And glass protect observer
And observed. The ledge

Of rocks defends their dignity
When lusts are obvious
And the dark throat bawls
For its keeper's pale meat.

Lank giraffes tread
Deliriously through heat—
At the edge of rage and sense
The eagle strains in truss.

Swimming

The eight of them were squatted along the beach
Before we even took notice. They were armed,
Or at least the man was, and we were in arm's reach.
But strange to say, we weren't just then alarmed.

Twenty of us, naked as worms, we swam
Just off the point and kept our laughing up
Until that skinny man began to ream
His piece: his first shot upstream was the slap

That caught us onto what the children wanted—
"Fun, fun, fun, fun!" they screamed. So did the wife.
We scrambled up our bank. My side chanted,
"Redneck, redneck . . ." Their man shot at our life.

Neither side was right: we should have played
The scared part, for the kids; they shouldn't
    have felt betrayed.

The Lawyer

It wasn't the Areopagus
Or even the sort of outdoor work
Some men are able to dignify—
Not what I found in the high field
The time I first checked on a murder
Witness. An old Negro was feeding
Chickens from a slot machine,
Poured grain down the top he'd pulled off
And out it came just like pure gold.
His cock and hens fought for the tray
While we got soaked by a slow March rain . . .
It wasn't the legal profession I'd sought.

He'd been known to help out before.
You went to where he was when the rest
Who'd seen the whole damn thing were deaf,
Blind, dumb and innocent as Fudgsicles.
They said once he'd kept his eyes and tongue
For twenty dollars when both sides died.
But on my day he wasn't selling.

I stood there in wet chickenshit
And shot back something about the law
And *how the hell was justice done* . . . ?
But his eyes were queer as my law was.
He wasn't rude like the new ones.
He thanked me for my offering
But said there wasn't profit in it;
So I figured he'd been talked to,
Had gotten straight just what the game was
And knew his side. I left his rooster
Winning every time, and felt
More out of place than his machine.

His Old Friend Who Sometimes Comes to Talk

In May, his last time over, he drank too much,
Was vulgar and sick by one, then wept till three—

It was all about the end of such and such
An order, but I never follow well the free
Confusion of the graceful past not memory

And I honestly suspect mortality
In general defeats him more than Lee.

The Politician's Pledge

You'd think there was heat enough all day,
With the sun the whole white sky—
But in my counties they burn things down
At night. No cool Christ in the tomb
Will do for them. They thrive on fire,
And I'll be damned if I'll feed fire.
Preachers! It's preachers I always blame.
They whine in the dusk for Zion's flames.

Make me an out-of-work mechanic
And bring my whole family down sick
If I ride one nigger again.
When it comes time for me to run
My tongue is ice—
Conditioned air in every house—
And if for that I'm not sent back,
I hope they're resurrected black.

On Hearing That the State Economic Council
Believes $5000 a Year for Every White Family
Will Quiet Things Down

There are pink flamingos
On metal legs in their yard
And grass is growing
Where once it was beaten hard—

There's a border of tire
Halves painted white
Where last year
Most blacks wouldn't walk at night.

Eden's Threat

Still now, at the brake's edge,
   we stand, confused by the sun.

All that time! Years
   it must have been, and the gunfire
   along the bayous was not so bright
   as this day is . . .

Years on the dead run,
   the hounds near—then hidden
   at night in dim pine shacks
   with a lank, soft woman—

We touch our stubble faces,
   the lean bones of our chins,
   and we were never caught
   and Eden's threat is less
   where we have been.

Miracle Play

Jonathas who stabbed the Host in the ancient play
And got God's blood was fortunate, though he lost
His soul awhile.
      To think of that and the way
His doubt was healed by Christ Himself could weigh
Upon your reverie, could cause alarm
At night, when the day's hand is ripped from its arm—
When the cauldron's stew you know is you seems sin
At best . . .
      In fact, you'd hope to Hell
It *is* sin you feel . . .
      For if it's not, then the flesh you smell
Remains in the mass a common human waste,
And the god's grace to the Medieval Jew
Is the wink of history, not prophecy.

Tornadoes (for H.R.T.)

Mine wasn't as extraordinary as
My grandfather's. His came down from higher,
A classical shape, hung from the Kansas sky.
Mine stooped over the woods, a squatty cloud.
Grandfather's, like a cornucopia
Gone haywire—sucking horribly, not spilling
Plenty (unless you grant the stories it left
A bounty)—came and beat his town down flat.

Hysterical naked women were in the streets;
Fortunes like his own were thrown across
The tragical Kansas plain, his jewelry store
A blasted treasure-trove.
              Every acre
In Kansas a sullen Populist demanding
His share—a pair of broken glasses, a diamond—
The grasses grown suddenly filthy rich,
And laughing—naked women howling all night—

His town become a waste on that rigorous land.
And he told that story each year, in still weather,
Until he died: Weeds! Diamonds gone!
And the neighbor's daughter turning around and around . . .

Mine came bucking over the trees and fell,
For a moment, to lift one dog, and that was all,
A helpless dog swung up in an awkward squall,
And nothing was beaten flat to raise a tale.

Just North of Sikeston

One night just north of Sikeston
I had a vision, or at least an insight,
Driving at fifty where before the worst
Was eyestrain. (It was within the legal limit.)

The season was spring and every truck and car
Had perfect manners, held
To their side and blinked their headlights
To keep from going blind—
A lovely thing when you think what could easily happen
On an eighteen-foot road with a lip
If people get a little out of line.
That brought the horrors, the vision,
    or what you will . . .
You see, I realized some mean to die—
Some, too much aware
Of spring and how the earth
Begins to hate them less, will fling themselves
And families across the median.
With the weather getting better, these winter men
Will cram one lane with life
To quiet the ugly wife
And free themselves and children from the long ways
I want to ride with mine for years. Dear God,
I thought, please let him kill in some other state

Tonight, as he seems to . . .
Or, better, let him die
Alone in a ploughed field,
His throat slit by his own hand—
Or in a big motel,
His pistol in his mouth—
Don't let him crush his family, or mine,
Or any other man's. Save, if you can,
A dozen lives too subtle to abide
A fury of metal. Let
No man gone out of round tear living years
On a wheel insanely rolling bloody from
The berm. It's love that dims
Our lights. It's praise that we take care to ease
Ourselves from every curve.

Notes for a Homily: The Medieval Monk Broods Over an Epic

A better ending would be for the hero to have a great illumination immediately after killing the dragon.

In that moment of light he would know that the dragon had been trying to protect him from the treasures, and that all the huffing and puffing had been because the poor beast believed that dramatics were the only thing a hero could understand.

If the hero realized this, he would have such a great sense of compunction that he would bury the dragon *and* the treasures.

He would say nothing about the fight with the dragon and he would say nothing about the treasures.

He would put an end to one curse.

Leavings

I hesitate to enter rooms
Where friends intend to be themselves;
I find myself afraid of wives
Who never mention sex until
Their husbands have gone to pee. But still
I move right in among those breasts
They say are only for baby. If

I run I'll never understand
Illogical tales, bad jokes, and men
Who horrify themselves until
They leave marks on public walls.

It's impossible to tell until
You've been. You have to go beyond
Dead Ends, on down below the sign
Into the brake, to find the wrack

Of something that lived—the hide of a cow
Caught in the vines, the hollow ribs
Of birds dried on the sand, or what
Remains of the child they say was murdered
Fifteen years ago. You have
To go in there to see if leavings
Are wastes and void of common truth.

Kalma

Kalma, "odor of the corpse," is the word
  for death with Finns, and in one myth they say
  the soul and the blood are one: they weep at graves,
  make offerings before decay. And I've heard

Finn warriors will eat the heart and the lungs
  of their dead to win the spirit back, to hold
  those best remains from the earth and the cold
  they know so well.

Yet they have no hell.

For a Neighbor Child

I yelled at you for climbing too high in our tree
and descents like death confuse the memory
and your falling face won't go and something more—
the awful order of the past must be
the necessary lie . . .

Up there at twelve you turned to kiss my son
and now all's dark and you are younger than he.
You had such courage, climbed the tree and fell—
fell through limbs down thirty silent feet
and all the age you'd learned . . .

And then you slept before you died
and I have had to say you dreamed he'd fallen too . . .
I could not miss your breaking skull
and the few leaves your lover saw follow
and you are constant in that fall . . .

A film in time continues to snap you up and down,
a terrible reel that holds me still,
for I praised when he wept against us great tears.

My Son's Bad Dreams

Usually he wears his mother's
  lovely manners
And carries himself as I do
  when I get my way.
He goes well with our friends, and to hear
  his regular teachers
He is wonderful
  at study and play . . .

But some nights he flounders and whines
  in a sweaty bed:
He has caught the factitious fever
  from his mother,
And from me he knows he will soon
  need more than water—
He cries out how his good days
  fill him with dread.

My Elderly Cousin (for F.S.)

In the thirties she saw three men shot down
My elderly cousin
The family's only painter,
And once in Chicago Grant Wood went for her knee.
She hardly understood
The thirties, and maybe Wood was lonely.

She paints great plains whereon there are no men
Except for her coarse father, her railing mother.
Her scapes are vicious with color—
Chartreuse Nebraska skies
Impasto vermilion stalks
No one has ever believed, and only orange hawks
For animals about that odd land sea.

I ask her to talk more of the thirties. "I'd rather
Forget the cities now," she says. Her hand
Whirls over her knee, describes her bad land.

One for the Sea

When eyes go blind or wild among the waves
The roads of water flame through corposants
And light all time remembered by the slaves
Of twenty senses from the bowels of saints,
Old zodiacs of wine and undead husks . . .

And that you say is too far gone for poetry
When of the modern tooling school. I

Have learned your way, to be exact, but fear
At times its hard lucidity, and hear
The furor of a larger, turbid time . . .

It's then I disremember style and the need
To grind verse fine, and sink my heart to the source . . .

This miraculous flailing sea recorded as culture
Is a storm of scalding salt, if I choose that course—
Or a passive beach where bodies rot, but stink not.

News Photo with a Hurricane Story

An image of a man and the wrack and the sea
and something about to be shot forced on me
a careful search.

At first I thought he shot
his hat, a strange thing to do in the rain;
then I realized the dark place was a coiled snake,
and felt I knew why a picture like that
was sent to state how it is when great storms break.

In awful weather, his gun's accusing line
and the name of his town and the date
of his natural crime
were witnesses to fear—
and I am sure his home washed out
when he fell in his hate to blast that thoughtless head . . .

But I can't laugh, though through gun-crack and spatter
he was so ignorant,
for few should unpersonify great pain
until the sea makes clear just what it means—
until the wind begins to explain, to explain, to explain . . .

Overcoming Bad Weather

The wind had ripped off the roof of the R.E.A.
and the American Legion, too—there's still some justice—
or balance—or at least what's indiscriminate
continues. Rough weather all around. High water—
and of an afternoon I was leaving home
awhile to journey alone away from children
and passed the heavy cover of a sewer
that spouted two spews from its little furious holes,
geysers that were not at all baroque. High wind—

I was driving our brand new car so carefully
to balance the bottle of bourbon properly
between my legs on the floor, that it not fall down at all;
and it didn't, though I passed a flattened home
with underwear everywhere on the trees and the lawn
and passed mysterious girls, frenzied in puddles,
and compassionate politicians cleaning fish.

It sat so well erect I thought
I'd overcome bad weather and
the babble of my own dear spawn
and the romantic mounds
of water rising beneath the street . . .

I drove as if I were a galleon
and drove as if it were a kind of fun
with the fifth on the floor—and it certainly never fell
as I passed those fountains of children, and raw clouds,
and distances I'd never known
until I crashed and burned in the sun.

First Lecture

Recently I heard a friend was mad.
It seems he took to women by the score,
Went nude to teach a class of freshmen boys,
Then burned the books he loved.
No doubt this fits
Some classic case concluded and almost cured
Years ago. But I won't seek a paradox
To call him sane.
He was no Christ, and his loss
Of mind might well have led to serious crime.

He was the kind we rarely understand.
He feared the voice, was pressed to complete a clause
Without a breath—
His lungs were strong, but he weighed
Each word too carefully . . .
He knew nine languages
By heart and tried to read each line of poetry
As if it were the last the man had said.
He wanted to know what caused a hand to push pen
Or to type, he wanted to know why any man
Felt wise enough to speak
At all. This led to his fall.

Yet now they say he rests quite well,
Takes easily to therapy,
Though they have no plans to let him out,
And I hear he reads again for his board,
He reads to children and the old,
Will keep it up so long as they
Will stay and at this play all seem
To understand, for none require
The meaning of a word he reads,
And his stammering has almost stopped . . .

Which brings to mind a thought he used to say:
The end of style for honest men is clarity.

On the Lady's Clothes

Beauty is a skirt.
It's not dull clothes
Of a boy on a lady's body—
Common cloth
Wound round and separating
Lovely legs,
Not hide and hair and that
Gruff coat that hangs
To your bound knees.

Recollect the bright designs
Suggesting where
A hand with ease begins
Some transport from
The rigorous world of men,
Release again
Fantastic shapes I fear—
Make them loose and soft
And terribly easy and near.

Let me unburden you
Of this harsh array—
I've dressed you supple skins
For rare display.

Cul-de-sac

My mother lost a child while I was twelve, but it wasn't
the way it was yesterday when my love did. My mother's
loss had a sex and was my brother a day, for he breathed
awhile before he died. And I cried he hadn't had a chance,
which was true, abashed to see him dressed in blue in his
neat box.

O he was wax, a sullen doll, and there was a preacher too
(and a grave for his birth), saying he'd be near God's
throne in spite of Catholics who give the cul-de-sac
to such as he.

But it was not that way yesterday when our flesh was stooled
or so we guess, for what I brought in the jar was after-
birth and the cord, the doctor said.

Words for the Sexual Revolution

Such exercise over your grandfather's way
Of making love—simply because you say
He never filled your Granny's *needs*. Maybe so . . .

But it seemed the thing to do when he felt like it
Or not at all—slowly, when spring came late,
Then like a hog to fit the autumn weather.

After such, they'd sleep for hours. Don't shout.
Be patient and let them die without assault.
Let their style break down like the maiden aunt who recalled

In perfect clarity, after twenty years,
The thing she said that set it wrong and sent
Her lover sadly away. She fumbled up

To her bed, turned out the lamp and buried her head
For fifteen more. Her groans, doctors smiling,
And echoes of heavy breathing from grandfather's room

Have breached these old walls whereon you strain your hate . . .
Only a damned fool would try to muscle a dead weight.

Love Poem in Midwinter

Herein is praise for your nose
As fine as a collie's,
Praise and the famous
Silent whistle. Please

Come back in those glossy, bestial
Boots—hard legs
You've fringed with fur.
You can trust a man who begs.

For MM

I cried. It was that simple
Except for feeling like a fool
With all those tears for a blonde.
Then I felt I ought to cry more.
She lived with fear and tried

For innocence. And we mustn't
Laugh at what she dreamed—
It seems she was standing nude in church
A sacrifice for all
Her guilt and ours, which means she loved
Uncommonly. For this
And all her comedy I write—

I offer praise because
She was the way we wanted her—
Magnificent goat without stench.
And I pray the earth on her
Is gentler than our hands.

Walking Around

My dear, your buttocks shift
Diastole, systole,
They pump like a lecher's heart—

And as you move away
I praise each lady's pulse,
Each muscle of this day.

For the Lady at Her Mirror

Begin by brushing hair,
Begin the easy strokes one hundred times
And say the rime to the mirror,
And hide your hands against your eyes where lines—
A few—have taught despair.

You are a Foolishness—broken up
With vessels in the thighs
And suffering beneath the chin to pat
And pat. Your long flesh abides,
The honest bait, the ancient prop and pit . . .

Go on, Lady, fear
The fall. Fear every change of color
And pressure—but when I am near
Take growing pleasure in every cunning cover
That binds our love and common disrepair.

Domains

1

Sometimes I find it hard to concentrate
On politics
And the rugged Brotherhood of Man—
I mean to be a Populist
Who goes according to a good reformer's plan
With all the races for a swim . . .
And the local union gets my dues . . .
But still the pamphlets, tracts and speeches bring the blues
And dreams of flight
To Red and Yellow, Black and White
Who tumble on the common beach
And by wild water where
The common terror will be shared.

2

This is the way a young man has to learn . . .
Making love to economics and the faithless moon.

3

One great-great-grandfather died
At twenty-seven of rotten meat that carried worms

In the Civil War
For the Union—
But on the other side
Dr. Bourland suffered Vicksburg
Lived to write a book to state the wisdom of his life
And cried when his eyes went out.

4

I stagger with my banner everywhere
Toward a better state
But always lovely hair
Long limbs negotiate
To turn my mind from taxes
And jack the old reflexes.

5

It is all death in time I would obliterate
And rigorous confusions of the noble dead—
But be it flesh, or memory,
Or present justice in a rout,
God, give me strength to nervously admit
I am not fit
To serve at once
Two dying bodies with equal wit.